Summer Food

Everyday recipes to enjoy

mozzarella salad with sun-dried tomatoes

ingredients

SERVES 4

140 g/5 oz sun-dried tomatoes in olive oil (drained weight), reserving the oil from the bottle

15 g/$1/2$ oz fresh basil, shredded coarsely

15 g/$1/2$ oz fresh flat-leaf parsley, chopped coarsely

1 tbsp capers, rinsed

1 tbsp balsamic vinegar

1 garlic clove, chopped coarsely

olive oil, if necessary

pepper

100 g/$31/2$ oz mixed salad leaves, such as oakleaf lettuce, baby spinach and rocket

500 g/1 lb 2 oz smoked mozzarella, sliced

method

1 Put the sun-dried tomatoes, basil, parsley, capers, vinegar and garlic in a food processor or blender. Measure the oil from the sun-dried tomatoes jar and make it up to 150 ml/5 fl oz with more olive oil if necessary. Add it to the food processor or blender and process until smooth. Season to taste with pepper.

2 Divide the salad leaves among 4 individual serving plates. Top with the slices of mozzarella and spoon the dressing over them. Serve immediately.

charred pepper salad

ingredients

SERVES 4–6

2 green peppers

2 red peppers

2 yellow peppers

1/2 tsp cumin seeds or 2 tbsp
    chopped fresh marjoram

5 tbsp extra virgin olive oil

2 tbsp lemon juice

2 garlic cloves, crushed

pinch of sugar

salt and pepper

Greek olives, to garnish

method

1 Preheat the grill. Grill the peppers, turning frequently, until the skins are charred all over. Put the peppers in a bowl, cover with a damp tea towel and leave until cold.

2 When the peppers are cold, hold them over a clean bowl to collect the juices and peel off the skin. Remove the stem, core and seeds and cut the peppers into thin strips. Arrange the pepper strips on a flat serving plate.

3 If using cumin seeds, dry-toast them in a dry frying pan until they turn brown and begin to pop. Shake the pan continuously to prevent them from burning and do not allow them to smoke. Lightly crush the toasted seeds with a pestle and mortar.

4 Add the toasted cumin seeds or marjoram, the olive oil, lemon juice, garlic, sugar, salt and pepper to the pepper juices and whisk together.

5 Pour the dressing over the peppers and chill in the refrigerator for 3–4 hours or overnight. Serve at room temperature, garnished with olives.

orange & olive salad

ingredients

SERVES 4

4 thick-skinned oranges

1 small red onion, sliced
    very thinly

16 large black Greek olives,
    pitted

2 tbsp extra virgin olive oil

1 tbsp lemon juice

pinch of sugar

salt and pepper

lettuce leaves, to serve

chopped fresh herbs such
    as flat-leaf parsley, mint
    or dill, to garnish

method

1 Using a sharp knife, remove the peel and pith from the oranges, then cut the flesh into 5 mm/$\frac{1}{4}$ inch thick slices, discarding the seeds and white membrane. Put the oranges and any juice, onion slices and olives in a large bowl.

2 To make the dressing, whisk together the oil, lemon juice, sugar, salt and pepper and drizzle over the salad ingredients. Gently toss together, then chill in the refrigerator for 2–3 hours.

3 Serve in a shallow dish lined with lettuce leaves. Garnish with chopped fresh herbs.

tabbouleh

ingredients

SERVES 4

175 g/6 oz bulgar wheat

3 tbsp extra virgin olive oil

4 tbsp lemon juice

salt and pepper

4 spring onions

1 green pepper,
    deseeded and sliced

4 tomatoes, chopped

2 tbsp chopped
    fresh parsley

2 tbsp chopped fresh mint

8 black olives, stoned

chopped fresh mint,
    to garnish

method

1 Place the bulgar wheat in a large bowl and add enough cold water to cover. Let stand for 30 minutes, or until the wheat has doubled in size. Drain well and press out as much liquid as possible. Spread out the wheat on kitchen paper to dry.

2 Place the wheat in a serving bowl. Mix the olive oil and lemon juice together in a jug and season with salt and pepper. Pour the lemon mixture over the wheat and marinate for 1 hour.

3 Using a sharp knife, finely chop the spring onions, then add to the salad with the green pepper, tomatoes, parsley and mint and toss lightly to mix. Top the salad with the olives and garnish with the chopped mint, then serve immediately.

salad niçoise

ingredients

SERVES 4–6

2 tuna steaks, about 2 cm/
  3/4 inch thick

olive oil

salt and pepper

250 g/9 oz French beans,
  trimmed

2 hearts of lettuce, leaves
  separated

3 large hard-boiled eggs,
  cut into quarters

2 juicy vine-ripened tomatoes,
  cut into wedges

50 g/13/4 oz anchovy fillets
  in oil, drained

55 g/2 oz black olives

torn fresh basil leaves,
  to garnish

garlic vinaigrette

125 ml/4 fl oz olive or other
  vegetable oil

3 tbsp white wine vinegar or
  lemon juice

1 tsp Dijon mustard

1/2 tsp caster sugar

salt and pepper

method

1 To make the garlic vinaigrette, put all the ingredients in a screw-top jar, secure the lid and shake well until an emulsion forms. Taste and adjust the seasoning if necessary.

2 Heat a ridged griddle pan over a high heat until you can feel the heat rising from the surface. Brush the tuna steaks with oil, then place, oiled-side down, on the hot pan and chargrill for 2 minutes.

3 Lightly brush the top side of the tuna steaks with a little more oil. Use a pair of tongs to turn the tuna steaks over, then season to taste. Continue chargilling for a further 2 minutes for rare or up to 4 minutes for well done. Let cool.

4 Meanwhile, bring a saucepan of salted water to the boil. Add the beans and return to the boil, then boil for 3 minutes, or until tender-crisp. Drain the beans and immediately transfer them to a large bowl. Pour over the garlic vinaigrette and stir together, then set aside to cool.

5 To serve, line a platter with lettuce leaves. Lift the beans out of the bowl, leaving the excess dressing behind, and pile them in the centre of the platter. Break the tuna into large flakes and arrange it over the beans.

6 Put the hard-boiled eggs and tomatoes around the edge and arrange the anchovy fillets, olives and basil on the salad. Drizzle over the remaining dressing and serve.

lime chicken with mint

ingredients

SERVES 6

3 tbsp finely chopped
    fresh mint

4 tbsp honey

4 tbsp lime juice

salt and pepper

12 boneless chicken thighs

mixed salad, to serve

sauce

150 ml/5 fl oz low-fat thick
    plain yogurt

1 tbsp finely chopped
    fresh mint

2 tsp finely grated lime rind

method

1 Mix the mint, honey and lime juice in a large bowl and season with salt and pepper. Use cocktail sticks to keep the chicken thighs in neat shapes and add the chicken to the marinade, turning to coat evenly.

2 Cover with clingfilm and marinate the chicken in the refrigerator for at least 30 minutes. Remove the chicken from the marinade and drain. Set aside the marinade.

3 Preheat the grill to medium. Place the chicken on a grill rack and cook under the hot grill for 15–18 minutes, or until the chicken is tender and the juices run clear when the tip of a knife is inserted into the thickest part of the meat, turning the chicken frequently and basting with the marinade.

4 Meanwhile, combine all the sauce ingredients in a bowl. Remove the cocktail sticks and serve the chicken with a mixed salad and the sauce, for dipping.

greek-style beef kebabs

ingredients

SERVES 4–6

1 small onion, finely chopped

1 tbsp chopped fresh
   coriander

large pinch of paprika

1/4 tsp ground allspice

1/4 tsp ground coriander

1/4 tsp brown sugar

450 g/1 lb beef mince

salt and pepper

vegetable oil, for brushing

freshly cooked bulgar wheat
   or rice, and mixed salad,
   to serve

fresh coriander leaves,
   to garnish

method

1 If you are using wooden skewers, soak them in cold water for 30 minutes before use.

2 Put the onion, fresh coriander, spices, sugar and beef into a large bowl and mix until well combined. Season with salt and pepper.

3 On a clean work surface, use your hands to shape the mixture into sausages around skewers. Brush them lightly with vegetable oil.

4 Grill the kebabs over hot coals, turning them frequently, for 15–20 minutes, or until cooked right through. Arrange the kebabs on a platter of freshly cooked bulgar wheat and garnish with fresh coriander leaves. Serve with a mixed salad.

marinated lamb & vegetable kebabs

ingredients

SERVES 4

juice of 2 large lemons

100 ml/3½ fl oz olive oil, plus
    extra for oiling

1 garlic clove, crushed

1 tbsp chopped fresh oregano
    or mint

salt and pepper

700 g/1 lb 9 oz boned leg or
    fillet of lamb, trimmed and
    cut into 4-cm/1½-inch
    cubes

2 green peppers

2 courgettes

12 baby onions, peeled and
    left whole

8 large bay leaves

lemon wedges, to garnish

rice, to serve

cucumber & yogurt dip

1 small cucumber

300 ml/10 fl oz Greek-style
    yogurt

1 large garlic clove, crushed

1 tbsp chopped fresh mint
    or dill

salt and pepper

method

1 To make the cucumber and yogurt dip, peel then coarsely grate the cucumber. Put in a sieve and squeeze out as much of the water as possible. Put the cucumber into a bowl. Add the yogurt, garlic and chopped mint, season with pepper and mix thoroughly. Chill in the refrigerator for 2 hours. Sprinkle with salt just before serving.

2 Put the lemon juice, oil, garlic, oregano, salt and pepper in a bowl and whisk together. Add the lamb to the marinade.

3 Toss the lamb in the marinade, cover and refrigerate overnight or for at least 8 hours. Stir occasionally to coat the lamb.

4 When ready to cook, core and deseed the peppers, and cut into 4-cm/1½-inch pieces. Cut the courgettes into 2.5-cm/1-inch pieces. Thread the lamb, peppers, courgettes, onions and bay leaves onto 8 flat, oiled metal kebab skewers, alternating and dividing the ingredients as evenly as possible. Place on an oiled grill pan.

5 Cook the kebabs under a preheated grill for 10–15 minutes, turning frequently and basting with any remaining marinade. Serve hot, garnished with lemon wedges, with rice and the cucumber and yogurt dip.

grilled red snapper with garlic

ingredients

SERVES 6

2 tbsp lemon juice

4 tbsp olive oil, plus extra for
    greasing

salt and pepper

4 red snapper or mullet,
    scaled and gutted

2 tbsp chopped fresh herbs
    such as oregano,
    marjoram, flat-leaf parsley
    or thyme

2 garlic cloves, chopped
    finely

2 tbsp chopped fresh
    flat-leaf parsley

lemon wedges, to garnish

method

1 Preheat the grill. Put the lemon juice, oil, salt and pepper in a bowl and whisk together. Brush the mixture inside and on both sides of the fish and sprinkle on the chopped herb of your choice. Place on a greased grill pan.

2 Grill the fish for about 10 minutes, basting frequently and turning once, until golden brown.

3 Meanwhile, mix together the chopped garlic and chopped parsley. Sprinkle the garlic mixture on top of the cooked fish and serve hot or cold, garnished with lemon wedges.

lime-drizzled prawns

ingredients

SERVES 6

4 limes

12 raw king prawns, in their
   shells

3 tbsp Spanish olive oil

2 garlic cloves, finely
   chopped

splash of dry sherry

salt and pepper

4 tbsp chopped fresh
   flat-leaf parsley, to garnish

method

1 Grate the rind and squeeze out the juice from 2 of the limes. Cut the remaining 2 limes into wedges and reserve for later.

2 To prepare the prawns, remove the legs, leaving the shells and tails intact. Using a sharp knife, make a shallow slit along the underside of each prawn, then pull out the dark vein and discard. Rinse the prawns under cold water and dry well on kitchen paper.

3 Heat the olive oil in a large, heavy-based frying pan, then add the garlic and fry for 30 seconds. Add the prawns and fry for 5 minutes, stirring from time to time, or until they turn pink and begin to curl. Mix in the lime rind, juice and a splash of sherry to moisten, then stir well together.

4 Transfer the cooked prawns to a serving dish, season to taste with salt and pepper and sprinkle over the parsley. Serve piping hot, accompanied by the reserved lime wedges for squeezing over the prawns.

sunshine paella

ingredients

SERVES 4–6

1/2 tsp saffron threads

2 tbsp hot water

150 g/51/2 oz cod, rinsed

1.4 litres/21/2 pints simmering
fish stock

12 large raw prawns, shelled
and deveined

200 g/7 oz live mussels,
scrubbed and debearded

3 tbsp olive oil

150 g/51/2 oz chicken breast,
cut into bite-size chunks
and seasoned to taste

1 large red onion, chopped

2 garlic cloves, chopped

1/2 tsp cayenne pepper

1/2 tsp paprika

225 g/8 oz tomatoes, peeled
and cut into wedges

1 red pepper and 1 yellow
pepper, deseeded and
sliced

375 g/13 oz paella rice

salt and pepper

175 g/6 oz canned sweetcorn
kernels, drained

3 hard-boiled eggs, cut into
quarters lengthways,
to serve

lemon wedges, to serve

method

1 Put the saffron threads and water in a bowl and infuse. Cook the cod in the simmering stock for 5 minutes. Rinse under cold running water, drain, cut into chunks and set aside in a bowl. Cook the prawns in the stock for 2 minutes. Add to the cod. Discard any mussels with broken shells or that refuse to close when tapped. Add to the stock and cook until opened. Add to the bowl with the other seafood, discarding any that remain closed.

2 Heat the oil in a paella pan over medium heat. Cook the chicken, stirring, for 5 minutes. Add the onion and cook, stirring, until softened. Add the garlic, cayenne pepper, paprika and saffron and its soaking liquid and cook, stirring, for 1 minute. Add the tomatoes and peppers and cook, stirring, for 2 minutes.

3 Add the rice and cook, stirring, for 1 minute. Add most of the stock, bring to the boil, then simmer, uncovered, for 10 minutes. Do not stir during cooking, but shake the pan once or twice and when adding ingredients. Season, then cook for 10 minutes, or until the rice is almost cooked, adding more stock if necessary. Add the seafood and corn and cook for 3 minutes.

4 When all the liquid has been absorbed and you detect a faint toasty aroma coming from the rice, remove from the heat. Cover with foil and stand for 5 minutes. Serve topped with egg quarters and garnished with lemon wedges.

fusilli with courgettes, lemon & rosemary sauce

ingredients

SERVES 4

6 tbsp olive oil

1 small onion, sliced
   very thinly

2 garlic cloves, chopped
   very finely

2 tbsp chopped fresh
   rosemary

1 tbsp chopped fresh flat-leaf
   parsley

450 g/1 lb small courgettes,
   cut into 5-mm x 4-cm/
   $1/_4$-inch x $1^1/_2$-inch strips

finely grated rind of 1 lemon

salt and pepper

450 g/1 lb fusilli tricolore

4 tbsp freshly grated
   Parmesan cheese

method

1 Heat the olive oil in a large frying pan over medium–low heat. Add the onion and gently fry, stirring occasionally, for about 10 minutes until golden.

2 Raise the heat to medium–high. Add the garlic, rosemary and parsley and cook for a few seconds, stirring. Add the courgettes and lemon rind. Cook for 5–7 minutes, stirring occasionally, until the courgettes are just tender. Season with salt and pepper. Remove from the heat.

3 Cook the pasta in plenty of boiling salted water until tender but still firm to the bite. Drain and transfer to a warmed serving dish.

4 Briefly reheat the courgettes. Pour over the pasta and toss well to mix. Sprinkle with the Parmesan cheese and serve immediately.

toasted pine nut & vegetable couscous

ingredients

SERVES 4

115 g/4 oz dried green lentils

55 g/2 oz pine nuts

1 tbsp olive oil

1 onion, diced

2 garlic cloves, crushed

280 g/10 oz courgettes, sliced

250 g/9 oz tomatoes,
    chopped

400 g/14 oz canned artichoke
    hearts, drained and cut in
    half lengthways

250 g/9 oz couscous

500 ml/16 fl oz vegetable
    stock

3 tbsp torn fresh basil leaves,
    plus extra leaves to garnish

pepper

method

1 Put the lentils into a saucepan with plenty of cold water, bring to the boil and boil rapidly for 10 minutes. Reduce the heat, cover and simmer for 15 minutes, or until tender.

2 Meanwhile, preheat the grill to medium. Spread the pine nuts out in a single layer on a baking sheet and toast under the preheated grill, turning to brown evenly – watch constantly because they brown very quickly. Tip the pine nuts into a small dish and set aside.

3 Heat the oil in a frying pan over medium heat, add the onion, garlic and courgettes and cook, stirring frequently, for 8–10 minutes, or until tender and the courgettes have browned slightly. Add the tomatoes and artichoke halves and heat through thoroughly for 5 minutes.

4 Meanwhile, put the couscous into a heatproof bowl. Bring the stock to the boil in a saucepan and pour over the couscous, cover and stand for 10 minutes until the couscous absorbs the stock and becomes tender.

5 Drain the lentils and stir into the couscous. Stir in the torn basil leaves and season well with pepper. Transfer to a warmed serving dish and spoon over the cooked vegetables. Sprinkle the pine nuts over the top, garnish with basil leaves and serve at once.

baked stuffed peaches

ingredients

SERVES 4

4 ripe peaches

4 tbsp unsalted butter

2 tbsp soft brown sugar

55 g/2 oz crushed amaretti or
   macaroons

2 tbsp Amaretto liqueur

125 ml/4 fl oz single cream,
   to serve

method

1 Prepare the peaches by cutting them in half and removing the stones (if you want to peel them, just dip them into boiling water for 10–15 seconds and then plunge them into cold water). Place the peaches cut sides up in an ovenproof dish greased with 1 tablespoon of the butter.

2 In a bowl, combine the remaining butter and sugar until creamy, then add the amaretti or macaroons and mix well. Stuff the peaches with the biscuit filling.

3 Bake in the centre of a preheated oven, 180°C/350°F/Gas Mark 4, for 20–25 minutes or until the peaches are soft. Pour over the liqueur and serve hot with the single cream.

lemon water ice

ingredients

SERVES 6

200 g/7 oz sugar

425 ml/15 fl oz water

6–9 large lemons

lemon slices, to decorate

method

1 Put the sugar and water in a heavy-based saucepan and heat gently, stirring, until the sugar has dissolved. Bring to the boil, then boil, without stirring, for 10 minutes to form a syrup. Do not let it brown.

2 Meanwhile, using a potato peeler, thinly pare the rind from 4 of the lemons. Remove the syrup from the heat and add the pared lemon rind. Cool for at least 1 hour.

3 Squeeze the juice from the lemons and strain into a measuring cup – you need 425 ml/15 fl oz in total. When the syrup is cold, strain it into a bowl, add the lemon juice and stir together until well mixed.

4 If using an ice cream maker, churn the mixture in the machine following the manufacturer's instructions. Alternatively, freeze the mixture in a freezerproof container, uncovered, for 3–4 hours or until mushy. Turn the mixture into a bowl and stir with a fork or beat in a food processor to break down the ice crystals. Return to the freezer and freeze for a further 3–4 hours or until firm. Cover the container with a lid for storing. Serve decorated with lemon slices.

This edition published in 2013
LOVE FOOD is an imprint of Parragon Books Ltd

Parragon
Chartist House
15–17 Trim Street
Bath, BA1 1HA, UK

www.parragon.com/lovefood

ISBN: 978-1-4723-0571-8

Printed in China

Notes for the Reader
This book uses both metric and imperial measurements. Follow the same units of measurement throughout; do not mix metric and imperial. All spoon measurements are level: teaspoons are assumed to be 5 ml, and tablespoons are assumed to be 15 ml. Unless otherwise stated, milk is assumed to be full fat, eggs and individual vegetables are medium, and pepper is freshly ground black pepper. Unless otherwise stated, all root vegetables should be washed in plain water and peeled prior to using.

For best results, use a food thermometer when cooking meat and poultry – check the latest government guidelines for current advice.

Garnishes, decorations and serving suggestions are all optional and not necessarily included in the recipe ingredients or method.

The times given are an approximate guide only. Preparation times differ according to the techniques used by different people and the cooking times may also vary from those given. Optional ingredients, variations or serving suggestions have not been included in the time calculations.

Recipes using raw or very lightly cooked eggs should be avoided by infants, the elderly, pregnant women, convalescents and anyone suffering from an illness. Pregnant and breastfeeding women are advised to avoid eating peanuts and peanut products. Sufferers from nut allergies should be aware that some of the ready-made ingredients used in the recipes in this book may contain nuts. Always check the packaging before use.